IT'S OUR GARDEN

From Seeds to Harvest in a School Garden

GEORGE ANCONA

CANDLEWICK PRESS

To Miss Sue

First paperback edition 2015

Library of Congress Cataloging-in-Publication Data is available.

Library of Congress Catalog Card Number 2012942313

ISBN 978-0-7636-5392-7 (hardcover)
ISBN 978-0-7636-7691-9 (paperback)

18 19 20 APS 10 9 8 7 6 5 4

Printed in Humen, Dongguan, China

This book was typeset in Diotoma.

Candlewick Press
99 Dover Street
Somerville, Massachusetts 02144

visit us at www.candlewick.com

INTRODUCTION

When I heard of schools having gardens, I became curious. So I went to visit some schools in Santa Fe, New Mexico, where I live. When I got to the Acequia Madre Elementary School, I stopped looking. Under the guidance of teachers, volunteers, and parents, children from kindergarten to sixth grade spend part of their day working in the garden behind the school building. The school is named for the four-hundred-year-old irrigation ditch across the street. (In Spanish, *acequia* means "irrigation ditch," and *madre* means "mother.")

The school is small. Entering the school seemed like entering a home. Outside, behind the school, the shouts from the playground drifted over the quiet children doing chores in the garden. I spent the better part of a year watching and photographing them as they worked side by side with their teachers, parents, and friends.

The school bell sounds . . .

and the classrooms explode with the
noise of books closing, chairs sliding
on the floor, and kids chattering. It's time
for recess! The students head outside to
the school garden.

Mrs. McCarthy (above), the third-grade teacher, dreamed of having a school garden. She talked to the other teachers, the principal, and the parents, and they all worked together to make her dream come true. The garden is cared for by Miss Sue (right).

Miss Sue's husband, Will, designed the layout of the garden. College students Paul, Danielle, Autumn, and Allie volunteer to guide the children in the garden projects.

Students enter the garden through an arbor. It's spring, and there are lots of chores to be done. Depending on the weather, some classes are held in the open classroom, the garden, or the greenhouse.

In early spring, Miss Sue asks the students to make a book with pictures they cut out from seed catalogs. These are the flowers, fruits, and vegetables that the students would like to grow. Later, she and the students will decide where to plant them.

Every day, one student is asked to take a bucket of food scraps from lunches and snacks and dump it into the compost pile.

The compost is made up of soil, dead plants, and food scraps. Inside the pile, red wriggler worms are busy eating and turning these ingredients into castings, which the students call poop. Compost is mixed into the garden beds to provide food for seedlings.

pinto beans

sunflower seeds

Springtime is planting time.
These are a few of the seeds
that will be planted in
the garden.

cucumber seeds

seed potatoes

When it's still cold outside, some seeds are planted in the greenhouse. There, students fill small plastic pots with rich soil and plant a seed in each. The pots are left in the greenhouse, where the sun warms them. Soon, tiny seedlings begin to pop out of the soil. When they are bigger and the weather is warmer, the plants will be transplanted into the garden beds outside.

Flowers, vegetables, and fruits are planted in the beds of rich composted earth. A tepee made of bamboo poles stands in the middle of the garden. Some students plant pole-bean seeds at the base of each pole. The plants will grow up the tepee and sprout their pods.

Meanwhile, in the morning shade of the school, Paul hands out salad-green and flower seeds to plant in a waffle bed. The bed's low walls of adobe bricks help keep water in.

Tomatos

Another group of students plants squash seedlings. Danielle helps a student transplant a tomato seedling. Once the seeds and seedlings are in the ground, the beds are watered and covered with a mulch of straw to keep the soil from drying out.

A lot of water is needed to keep the garden healthy. When it rains, water flows off the roof, down a drainpipe, and into an underground tank called a cistern. A solar panel on the roof of the outdoor classroom creates electricity to run the pump that draws water from the cistern. One of the students' favorite jobs is watering the garden. Miss Sue fills the colorful watering cans for them.

The tomato plants are surrounded by plastic tubes filled with water. During the day, the sun warms the water in the tubes. At night, the tubes provide the warmth that tomato roots need to grow. When there is no rain-water in the cistern, a hose attached to an outdoor faucet is used to keep the soil moist and plants healthy.

Even when the students aren't at school, there's a lot going on in the garden. A post with holes drilled into it becomes a nesting box for mason bees, which don't sting. Birds come to eat at the feeders. Worms are busy eating and making tunnels in the compost pile.

Flowers produce a sweet liquid called nectar. When a bird, a bee, or a butterfly goes into a flower to drink the nectar, a powder called pollen sticks to them. When they fly into another flower, the pollen rubs off. Pollen allows the flower to make the seeds that will grow into flowers, fruits, or vegetables. This process is called pollination.

In the early spring, a teacher orders butterfly cocoons by mail. When they arrive, the students put the cocoons in a net cage to raise them in the classroom. When the butterflies emerge, they are taken to the garden and released so they can pollinate the plants.

Many different creatures live in the garden or come by to visit. Crickets, ladybugs, grasshoppers, and beetles fly, hop, or crawl about.

Pill bugs, also called roly-polies, gophers and even garter snakes, can be found living among the garden's plants or tunneling in its soil.

Garden Observations 5/6/10 1st Grade

BiBi wintr HeLo
spring.

The apLchene troe or
BLooming.

The Laty Baugs
and dutter flis anad
Beas or Bac.
The Sen is Shining.

a tre is
aroweing

by:
Marina

1'st.
grad

There are lots of things in the garden to write and draw about. An easel in the middle of the garden invites anyone to draw what they see or write down their thoughts and experiences.

Some students use leaves to make leaf prints. Their art decorates the greenhouse and the outdoor classroom.

While the plants are growing during the warm spring days, there is still a lot of work to do in the garden. Students mix sand, dirt, water, and cut-up straw to make adobe bricks. The bricks are used to make the low walls for waffle beds. In the Southwest, adobe bricks are still used to build homes.

Digging

Adobe is also used to coat the *horno*, the traditional oven used to bake bread. Every spring, the *horno* in the corner of the outdoor classroom gets a fresh coat of adobe.

There are many different plants in the herb garden, such as basil, tarragon, lemon balm, chives, sage, lemon verbena, and Egyptian walking onions. Every plant has its own taste and smell.

Radishes are harvested in the spring. Miss Sue asks some students to pick the radishes. After washing the dirt off them, the children bite into the bright-red vegetables. One girl finds hers too spicy and drops it into the compost pile. More food for the worms!

On special afternoons and weekends, the garden becomes a place where the school community gathers. Students come back with their parents, sisters, brothers, grandparents, and friends. They compost, seed, plant, transplant, weed, water, and dig. By now, the flowers are blooming and the beds are green. The garden is flourishing with so much care.

hollyhock

Garden chores continue into summer. School is closed, but the garden is a beehive of activity. It provides the setting for music and gatherings of children, grown-ups, friends, and families. The music fills the garden with joy.

By August, many of the fruits and vegetables are ripe. Cooking and eating becomes an ongoing activity in the garden.

A father helps the children make pizzas on one community day. First they mix and punch the dough. Then they roll it out with a rolling pin and pour oil on the flat dough. Ripe tomatoes are cut up and go on top. And last, of course, is the grated cheese.

After a hot fire burns down in the *horno*,
the coals are leveled and the pizza goes in.
When the sizzling pizza is taken out, a group
of hungry gardeners appears. The slices
disappear like magic. Fortunately, there are
many more pizzas to come.

Bean teepee

Summer is over, and another school year begins. The leaves on the trees are turning color, and many of the garden's fruits and vegetables are ready to be picked. Students take turns disappearing into the tepee to pick pole beans from the vines.

One of the garden beds was planted in a traditional Native American way; it's called a three-sisters garden. Corn is planted together with pinto beans and squash. The bean vines grow up the cornstalks. The corn and squash leaves shade the soil to keep it moist. Pinto beans are harvested after the pods dry up and turn tan.

By September, most of the tomatoes are ripe.
Each student is given a limit as to how many they
can pick so there are enough left for later classes.
As the fall goes on, the days start getting cooler.
Some of the tomatoes are still green. Allie shows
the students how to ripen green tomatoes by
putting them into a paper bag with a banana.

Please don't pick
me. I need to
grow! Thanks,
                The
                tomato

putatose

leefs

Stem

rots

Miss Sue shows some children how to harvest potatoes. Using a shovel or a trowel, the students carefully dig down next to the stem. Since potatoes spread out as they grow, digging must be done carefully so that the shovel does not cut into them. Later, Allie helps them identify the different kinds of potatoes they have harvested.

Cabbages are a real challenge
to pick. Their long, strong roots
test the strength and stamina of
some of the bigger kids.

Lemon cucumbers, also called apple cucumbers, are a new experience for most of the students. The children like them because they can be eaten like apples.

In the three-sisters garden, the strawberry corn is ready for harvesting. The ears are taken off of the stalks, husked, and the kernels picked off the cob and saved in a jar.

Later, the kernels are heated in oil and turned into a delicious popcorn snack, much to the students' delight.

The harvest becomes a chance for Miss Sue to quiz the students on the variety of crops the garden has produced. She makes a game of the quiz, placing the answers facedown on slips of paper under each fruit, vegetable, or herb.

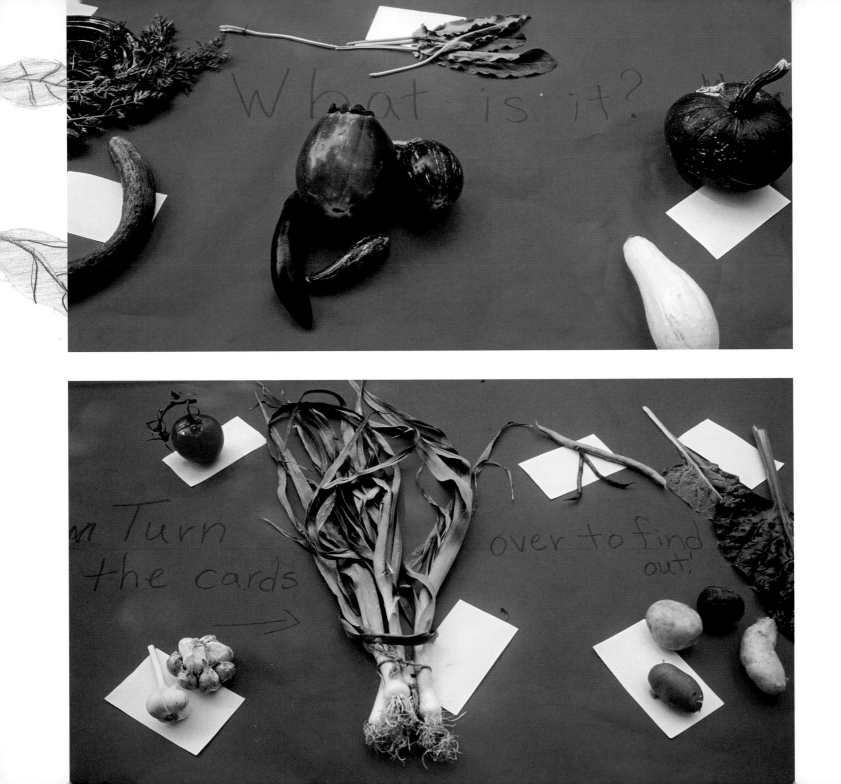

To celebrate the end of the harvest,
a series of lunches is prepared
with many of the garden's vegetables.
These become festivals of good
food and fun.

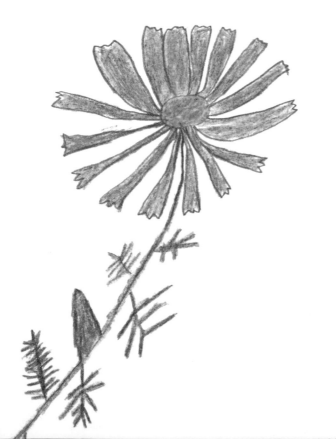

The last community day of the year brings students and families together to prepare the garden for winter. The air is crisp and cold. Frost has turned the trees to gold. Winds have scattered many leaves to the ground. The green plants of summer are shriveled and brown. Dead plants are yanked out of the ground and put into the compost pile.

Compost is strained
and mixed into the soil.
The strawberry plants and
beds are mulched with straw.
And all is ready to be covered
with a blanket of snow.
Sleep tight, garden!
Until next year!

TO ALL THE WONDERFUL PEOPLE WHO MADE THIS BOOK POSSIBLE:

To Sue McDonald, who graciously invited me to become a fixture in the garden, and her husband and co-creator, Will. To Barbara McCarthy and to the parents who made her dream come true. To the four moving forces in the garden: Paul Navrot, Danielle Simmons, Autumn Kern, and Allie Silber. To the principal, Mr. Bill Beacham, better known as Mr. B., and to the teachers, students, and parents of the Acequia Madre Elementary School, whose existence is a celebration of the history of this ancient city and the diversity of its people.

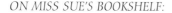

ON MISS SUE'S BOOKSHELF:

Aston, Diana Hutts. *A Seed Is Sleepy.* Illustrated by Sylvia Long. San Francisco: Chronicle, 2007.

Bunting, Eve. *Sunflower House.* Illustrated by Kathryn Hewitt. San Diego: Harcourt, 1996.

Cherry, Lynne. *How Groundhog's Garden Grew.* New York: Blue Sky, 2003.

Ehlert, Lois. *Eating the Alphabet.* San Diego: Red Wagon/Harcourt, 1996.

———. *Growing Vegetable Soup.* San Diego: Red Wagon/Harcourt, 2004.

———. *Planting a Rainbow.* San Diego: Harcourt, 1988.

Elschner, Géraldine. *Max's Magic Seeds.* Illustrated by Jean-Pierre Corderoch. New York: Penguin, 2007.

Gibbons, Gail. *From Seed to Plant.* New York: Holiday House, 1991.

Heller, Ruth. *The Reason for a Flower.* New York: Grosset & Dunlop, 1983.

Rabe, Tish. *On Beyond Bugs.* Illustrated by Aristides Ruiz. New York: Random House, 1999.

Richards, Jean. *A Fruit Is a Suitcase for Seeds.* Illustrated by Anca Hariton. Brookfield, CT: Millbrook, 2002.

SCHOOL GARDEN WEBSITES:

Acequia Madre School Garden
http://acequiamadregarden.org

Center for Ecoliteracy
http://ecoliteracy.org

CitySprouts
http://www.citysprouts.org

The Edible Schoolyard Project
http://edibleschoolyard.org/berkeley/about-us

Life Lab
http://www.lifelab.org

REAL School Gardens
http://realschoolgardens.org

San Francisco Green Schoolyard Alliance
http://sfgreenschools.org